Ripley and Send

LOOKING BACK

Surrey Village Life

&

its People

1890's ~ 1940's

Newark Priory.

Send & Ripley History Society
Surrey

The cover photograph shows Sally Edgell
on her donkey cart out scavenging
C 1900

First published 1987
© Send & Ripley History Society 1987
Send & Ripley History Society
Send Manor
Ripley
Surrey
GU23 6JS.

ISBN 0 9509961 2 2

Typeset and Printed by Lyndhurst Printing Company Limited,
Hardley Industrial Estate, Hythe, Southampton SO4 6ZX

Printed in England

Foreword

"Looking Back", a companion volume to "Then and Now", is an attempt to capture by photographs some sense of the enormous change in the way of life from the 1890's to the 1940's experienced by our parents and grandparents. We have tried to give a balanced picture of the working lives, the transport, the entertainments and the general pattern of life in these two Wey Valley villages.

The Victorian and Edwardian photographers did not often consider everyday life and work as suitable subjects for their albums. The earlier popular cameras, such as the Box Brownie, caught the fleeting moment but rarely had the quality suitable for reproduction. Despite these limitations we hope to give some feeling of Send and Ripley as they were for those who did not know them, and bring back memories for those who know the scenes and some of the people in the pictures.

A pictorial record gives little hint of the wealth of reminiscences which we have had recounted to us:- the live eels, caught in the river Wey, hanging from hooks in the living room wall, still wriggling; the pride in keeping the kitchen range shining with black lead polish; the joy of receiving a silver threepenny piece when carol singing; the loss of one's shoes when chased from paddling in the horse trough; the volunteer fireman who fell into the farm midden.

We are indebted to many of the inhabitants of Send and Ripley for their willingness and patience in telling us their recollections and answering our questions, and for the loan of their family photographs to copy.

Wherever possible we have checked dates and facts from census returns, parish magazines and other records.

Jane Bartlett.

Acknowledgements

We thank the many residents of Send and Ripley for contributing photographs and reminiscences which have made the book possible, and the members of the Send and Ripley History Society on whose researches we have drawn.

We acknowledge the following organisations for permission to reproduce their pictures:

The Automobile Association (No. 27). Croydon Library (Nos. 47, 61). Esher Library (No. 20). Guildford Institute (Nos. 14, 71). Guildford Museum (Nos. 66, 67, 70). Send Cricket Club (No. 124). Mitcham Library (Nos. 77, 79, 126). Surrey Record Office (Nos. 1, 3). Surrey Archaeological Society (No. 88). Unwin Brothers Limited (Nos. 51, 52, 101, from their archives at the Surrey Record Office).

We thank the following individuals for the loan of their photographs: Mrs P. Aldridge (Nos. 95, 102, 105). Mrs R. Avery (Nos. 12, 129). Mrs C. H. Baker (Nos. 4, 128). Mr R. Baker (Nos. 65, 113). Mrs R. Baker (Nos. 18, 19, 108, 109). Mrs J. Bartlett (97, 98, 106, 107). Mr G. Best (Nos. 26, 118, 133, 141). Mr K. Bourne (No. 69). Mr L. Bowerman (Nos. 34, 76, 99). Mr D. Bromley (Nos. 54, 125). Mrs R. Brown (No. 83). Mr T. Buller (No. 122). Mrs D. Challen (Nos. 42, 55a, 74, 85). Mrs A. Charman (Nos. 31, 32, 37, 114, 121, 127, 131, 132). Mrs P. Clack (Nos. 13, 43, 73, 75, 81). Miss Colborne (No. 110). Mr P. Conisbee (No. 40). Mr J. D. Evershed (Nos. 17, 89, 90). Mr P. Giles (Nos. 35, 36, 41, 138). Mrs R. Giles (Nos. 57, 58, 59, 62, 63, 103). Mr. N. Grove (Nos. 68, 116). Mr W. Heath (No. 8). Mr F. Hookins (No. 53). Mr. B. Howard (Nos. 23, 24, 39). Mrs King (No. 78). Mr D. Lillywhite (Nos. 33, 112). Mrs M. Lynn (No. 30). Mr A. Marsh (Nos. 29, 82, 119, 123). Mrs M. Meech (No. 135). Mr K. Methold (No. 140). Mrs Monk (No. 64). Miss B. Nokes (Nos. 5, 28, 91, 139). Mrs G. R. Nuttall (Nos. 15, 111, 115, 130). Miss R. Onslow (Nos. 11, 25, 38, 92, 93). Miss A. K. Palmer (No. 87). Mr D. E. Penny (No. 120). Mrs D. Pullen (No. 50). Mrs M. Sex (Nos. 84, 136). Mrs I. Sopp (Nos. 55, 80, 86). Mrs J. Stephens (No. 22) Miss J. Stevens (Nos. 117, 134). Mrs E. H. Strange (No. 44). Mr R. Tidy (No. 60). Mrs W. Turks (Nos. 7, 10, 16, 21). Mrs J. Watson (Nos. 49, 104). Mr R. Whapshott (Nos. 56a & 56b).

Other photographs are from the collection of the Send & Ripley History Society.

The artist Frank Brown has drawn for us the sketch map on Page 6.

We thank Ken Bourne for the majority of the photographic work, also Ian Gaunt, Bernard Watts and John and Betty Pamplin; Jane and John Bartlett and Mavis Lake for collecting and compiling the material; Les Bowerman for checking and proof reading.

LOOKING BACK

1.

The 'New Times' coach outside the "Talbot" in 1895.

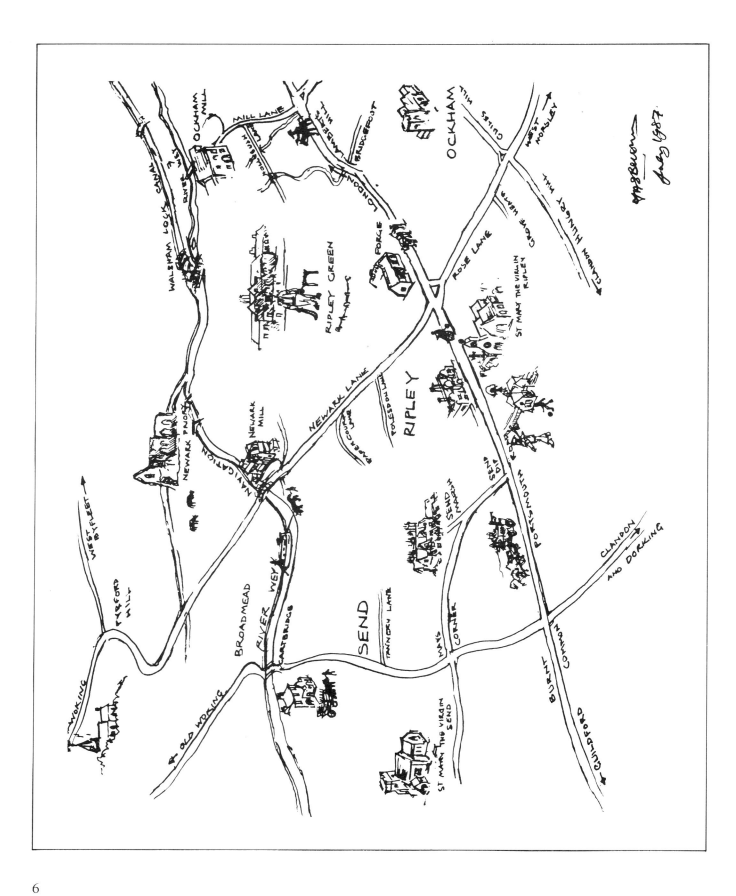

6

3.

Ripley was well known to travellers as it was on the coach route from London to Portsmouth. Horses were changed at the staging and posting inns, many of which are still there today – notably the "Talbot" and the "Jovial Sailor". A bustling busy High Street developed which is still recognisably the same as it was a hundred or more years ago, although some inns and shops have changed their use.

The last London to Portsmouth Mail Coach passed through Ripley in 1842, two years after the completion of the London to Southampton railway line, but there were still private carriages, road coaches and stage waggons passing through for several years. A coaching revival in the 1860s brought Walter Schoolbread's "New Times" coach from Piccadilly to Guildford. It is shown above changing horses at the "Talbot", a change which could be achieved in a matter of minutes.

4.

The 'Red Rover' once a regular sight in Ripley a hundred years before, was acquired and restored by Sanders Watney and is shown right passing the "White Hart" on its twice weekly run to Southampton in the period 1952-1965. It stopped at the "Jovial Sailor", and here the passengers were allowed a fifteen minute pause for tea.

COACH, CARRIAGE, CART.

Long after the coach traffic stopped there was still a great deal of horse traffic on the Portsmouth Road. Most shops had horse drawn delivery vehicles.

6.

Landaus, Brakes, etc. were still being advertised in the Parish Magazine in 1911.

5.

The census returns of 1881 give Stephen Green as cordwainer (shoe-maker) employing sixteen men, one boy and two women. His son, Richard, pictured in his tally cart, with Tommy Harding driving, expanded into clothing and furniture. He also started a second shop across the road for bicycles and ironmongery. His instalment system (tally) was a great boon in the days before credit cards. One old lady faced with buying an outfit for a wedding was heard to say "Mr. Green will see me all right".

7.

The delivery cart from Tedder's Store in 1910 with Mr. Pinnock on the right. Their rounds went far afield – to Pyrford, Wisley and Ockham where this picture was taken.

The Countess of Loveless frequently drove in her brougham (green with a yellow stripe) through the wrought iron gates at the London end of Ripley until the 1930s. Here it is with Cross the coachman. The stables can been seen behind.

8.

The carrier was an important personage listed in Kelly's directory. His carrier's cart was used to convey people to Guildford or to Clandon station, or on school outings. It was also used for transporting goods, delivering parcels, and furniture removing. On one occasion about 1912 he brought the school children back from their annual outing on the river. Unfortunately he had just been carting coal, and most of the girls wore white dresses! His horses were frequently borrowed by the Volunteer Fire Brigade when they were called to a fire.

Telegrams: *White, Ripley, Surrey.*   Telephone No. 9, Ripley

D. WHITE,
L. & S.W.R. Delivery Agent and Jobmaster,
FURNITURE REMOVER & STORER.
Landaus, Brakes, Waggonettes, etc. for Hire on the
Shortest Notice.

9.

Doug White and his cart in the celebrations at the end of the Boer War in 1902.

10.

11.

The Send/Woking horse bus was owned by Ernest Cox in 1910 and then by Sydney Brown. As well as carrying passengers it was used to deliver grocery orders sent out from the International and other stores in Woking, and to pick up parcels on the way.

It was usually quicker to walk, which many Send residents did daily to work or to do their shopping. "Do you want a lift?" "No thank you, I'm in a hurry" was frequently heard.

It was replaced in the '20s by a bus driven by 'producer' gas contained in a large balloon bag on the roof.

The Blue Saloon service from Guildford came later.

9

The blacksmith was very important. He shoed horses, repaired machinery, and he could even be persuaded to repair the kitchen range and the boys' iron hoops. The Ripley blacksmith was also wheelwright and farrier as well. He made medicines and ointments for horses and sometimes humans.

12.

Ripley forge about 1880.

13.

The Send blacksmith's C.H. Sex & Sons is now a garage like many other forges. It continued as a forge however until the 1960s, much later than most other village smithies, making wrought iron work famed all over the country, and even abroad. In the English church at Basle there is a fine example of a chancel screen made by them, and they also made the church gates at Montreux. But in 1929 horses still required shoeing as in this picture.

14.

With a good but empty turnpike road close to London, Ripley became the "Mecca of all good cyclists". Here in 1886 at the time of the Southern Counties Cyclists Camp held at Guildford, we can see members of the Dibble family outside the "Anchor" making cyclists welcome. This inn, rather than the "Talbot" was where they chiefly congregated and several hundreds would call there at the weekends.

15.

Richard Green's hardware shop in 1910 where bicycles were also sold and mended. It was later run by a relative, Charles Nokes, whose wife used to complain that the forefront of the shop and her cottage next door always looked cluttered with prams and bicycles.

16.

The boys of Ryde House School in 1904.

17.

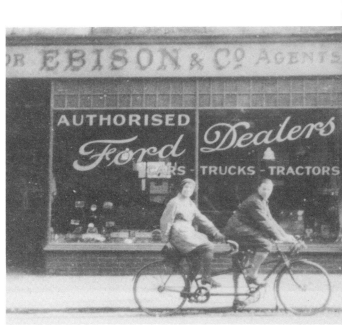

18.

By 1920 several local girls had joined the Woking section of the C.T.C. Although it was in 1898 that Lady Harberton, the President of the Western Rational Dress Association, was refused entry to the lounge of the "Hautboy" in her baggy knickerbockers called 'Rational Dress', Dolly Grace pictured here in her 1920s 'rationals' said they were still considered rather 'fast'.

19.

An outing to Wisley Common in 1916.

20.

THE PARISH BATH CHAIR.

"It has been felt for some time that it would be of great assistance to the sick and infirm if there were a bath chair available in the village for those who are permanently or temporarily incapacitated. Such a chair has now been procured by Mrs. Pearce, chiefly with the proceeds of the excellent entertainment given last spring by Flight-Sgt. B. Dibble and his concert party from Halton Camp, which were handed over to Mrs. Pearce for parochial purposes. This chair has been placed in the hands of the Vicar for the use of persons of all denominations. A fixed charge of 3d. a time will be made for the use of the chair. The money received will be placed in a fund to meet the cost of repairs and replacement of the chair when worn out."

Extract from Parish Magazine – November 1922.

21.

A picture of a cycle taxi taken by Frank Pinnock a keen local amateur photographer.

Mr. A. H. Lancaster outside the gates of Sendholme preferred another form of transport. The donkey was also employed in cutting the cricket pitch.

22.

FROM COACHING INNS TO CAFES.

The influx of visiting bicycles, followed in the 1920s by the visiting motor cars, caused a growth of tea-rooms. Mrs. Howard opened the Cedar House Tea Rooms in 1920 and she recalls that even on opening day the demand was such that food began to run out and visitors helped get their own tea. Many of the visitors became regulars – famous names such as Evelyn Laye, the Baddeley sisters, the Ramsay MacDonalds and Henry Ford all wrote their names in the visitors' book. The chef from the Metropole in Brighton always made his own omelette in the kitchen.

The rooms were furnished with antiques.

23.

24.

14

Other tea-rooms abounded, such as Skelton's Café and Pinnock's Café. Fairfield House, once a doctor's residence, became the Clocke House Restaurant. Later in the 1950s, S.P.B. Mais the writer and broadcaster, visited the Bright Spot (later the Green Lantern). He rejoiced over the two boiled eggs for tea, and the signed photographs of theatrical celebrities around the walls – among them those of Ellen Terry and the D'Oyly Carte Company.

25. Pinnocks Café

As Send was off the beaten track for the passing bicyclists and motorists it did not have tea rooms as such, but Mrs. Grove, wife of the Master Carpenter, used to cook chicken lunches for picnickers by the river near Worsfold Gates.

Mrs. Jarman, wife of the miller, and her sister Mrs. Best, opened a tea-room in a wooden hut near Newark Mill for those who came by boat or those who walked along the towpath. They were famed for their home made ice-cream. Here young George Best is showing off his new uniform in 1933.

26.

THE AGE OF THE CAR.

Early AA scouts, pictured outside the "Hut Hotel", Wisley in 1906, did their patrols on bicycles. There were very few cars on the roads and the speed limit was still 20 mph. After church and Sunday School the local children would stroll up the still fairly car-free Portsmouth road to the "Hut Hotel" and Bolder Mere.

27.

Charles Nokes who owned the hardware store, Richard Green Ltd., was usually in the forefront of new developments. He was one of the first owners of a crystal wireless set and one of the first in the village to charge batteries. Here on the right he is a proud owner in 1913 of one of the first cars in the village.

28.

This model T Ford, commonly known as 'Tin Lizzie', being pushed up Newark Lane, first belonged to Dr. Pearse, then Mr. Allenby the Chemist, and finally to Mr. Goodman, headmaster of Ryde House School. Mr. Spooner, Dr. Pearse's chauffeur, was delighted when he changed his pony and trap for a car. He had had many a long cold wait, as far afield as Horsley, while the doctor delivered a baby, and extra time had been spent in the morning and evening feeding the horse and harnessing the trap.

29.

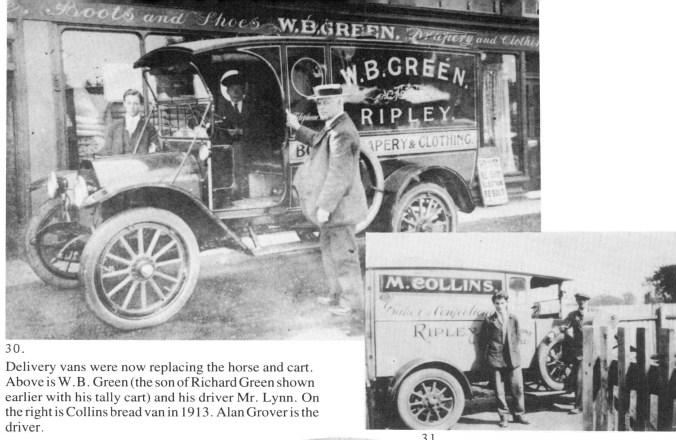

30.

Delivery vans were now replacing the horse and cart.
Above is W.B. Green (the son of Richard Green shown
earlier with his tally cart) and his driver Mr. Lynn. On
the right is Collins bread van in 1913. Alan Grover is the
driver.

31.

32.

A very large charabanc was needed to take a works outing down to Brighton in 1910. Standing on the right is Steve
Allwork with his nephew, Reg, at his side, and his other nephew, Charlie, directly above Reg. The Allworks who
were builders decorators and undertakers (and even at one stage started a school) employed a great many Ripley men.

33.

Premises were adapted to meet the changing times, and this in 1921 is Bland's garage. To make room for coaches to be kept at the back, the cottage on the left was bought and demolished. The coaches did a school run in the morning and took the workers to Vickers aircraft factory, and during the Second World War, in addition, they carried munitions to and from Vokes at Henley Park and brought the prisoners-of-war from the camp on Merrow Downs to work on local farms.

SHOPS.

34.
Not only was Ripley well provided with inns and cafés, its High Street had many long established shops.

There were at one time at least three bread shops. The one pictured on the right at the turn of the century is now Hartley Antiques.

36.

35.

37.

38.

This bread shop at the corner of Rose Lane has been baking bread since the 1850s and still does today. Mr. Peters is shown cutting raspings, with the dough machine just visible behind him. He worked here for 50 years for the Geales, the Collins, and Mr. Hewin. The village used him as an alarm clock as he set out every morning at 4 am to make the bread. He made the loaf for the Harvest Festival and cooked the Christmas turkey for many families until the 1930s. He felt he had to resign from the Volunteer Fire Brigade as sudden absences did not improve the bread.

There were also three butchers and two slaughter houses in Ripley at the turn of the century. This butcher moved to the opposite corner because of the expansion of the neighbouring Cedar Tea Rooms shown on page 14. The slaughter house was behind the shop in Rose Lane.

39.

Conisbee's butcher's shop, which has been in the family since 1905, today still supplies quality meat and poultry.

40.

Below, the second slaughter house is hidden behind Easton's shop. The village used to be filled with noise when the animals were driven up the street. There was great delight when one escaped pig was seen rushing back the way it had come with the slaughterman on its back. One of his jobs was to kill the cottagers' pigs in Send and Ripley – one they sold and one they kept for eating themselves. Note the sign-writer just replacing Bonner's name with that of Stevenson for the neighbouring shop.

41.

In contrast to the bustling well-provided High Street at Ripley, Send residents did their local shopping in the widely separated corner stores of their village.

42.

Webbs General Store and Bakery at Cartbridge was run by two brothers until the 1930s. The bachelor William Webb managed the shop while his brother, Jack, made the deliveries. It has been said that this picture is of Jack's horse taking refreshment from its nose-bag outside the "New Inn".

43.

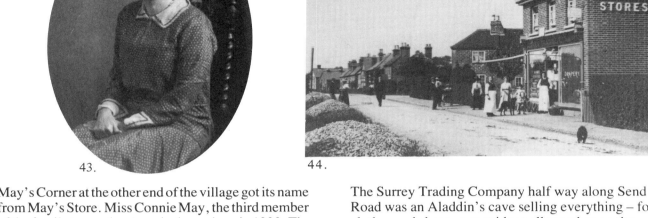

44.

May's Corner at the other end of the village got its name from May's Store. Miss Connie May, the third member of the family to run the store, is shown here in 1920. The children used to buy ginger beer with a glass alley in the neck of the bottle, and strips of liquorice on their way to school. Miss May let them pay with the tokens they received for strawberry picking which she would redeem for them.

The Surrey Trading Company half way along Send Road was an Aladdin's cave selling everything – food, clothes and shotgun cartridges all together on the counter, with saucepans, baskets, boots and mats hanging from the ceiling.

45.

Send Marsh Corner Store circa 1915. The car is believed to be that of a local doctor.

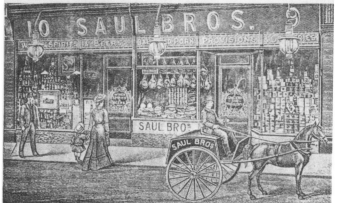

Many Send people however walked into Woking on Saturday when perishable goods were auctioned cheaply.

46.   Advertisement in the "Homeland Handbook" 1905.

47.

A special treat was going into Guildford, particularly on market day when a cattle market was held in North Street, and later in Woodbridge Road.

48.

Newark is probably the site of one of the two mills mentioned in the Domesday Survey of Send. It was given to Newark Priory in the 13th century by Thomas and Alice de Send. The final mill on the site was unique in having eight pairs of stones and three water wheels. The cogs were damaged in 1936 by debris in the water and flour ceased to be milled – only the coarser animal feed was ground – then sadly it was burnt down on 3rd December 1966. The old timber burnt very quickly and the heat was so intense that it charred the roof timbers of the neighbouring Newark Mill House through the slates.

Strangely enough the mill did not seem to have supplied the local shops within living memory – but barges carried flour, presumably to London, and Mr. Jarman delivered to Woking by lorry. It was Ockham Mill, pictured below with its miller Harvey Collins, which supplied Ripley with its flour, brought by waggon across the Green, and bought, amongst others, by his brother Maurice Collins the baker at the corner of Rose Lane.

49.

Send Tannery & Bridge, Woking

50.

INDUSTRY.

People can still remember the tannery workers with their skins stained yellow from the oak bark tannin. The locally grown bark came by barge. The raw hides came from Spain, producing very high quality leather which was sold in London. The tannery closed in 1929 when Johnny Ashford retired.

More recent memories are of peering into Mr. Hamburger's pulverising plant, Crack Processing Ltd., which took its place and seeing the sparkling bits of gum Arabic, or picking up and sucking pieces of liquorice which had dire effects on unsuspecting insides!

The Unwin Brothers printing works moved to the Broadmead site of the old paper mill in 1896 after their Chilworth factory had burnt down. Although many of their skilled workers walked in daily from Chilworth or Guildford, in time they were joined by local men giving a new occupation to the mainly rural area of Send. They built Gresham Gardens in Send Road as ideal homes for their workers.

Driven by the River Wey, the two turbines they installed kept up a constant hum. The river was an asset for their annual sports day when the slippery pole was poised over it, but it caused a problem to the work force when in spate and Unwins had to provide horses and carts to ferry them over the flooded Broadmead.

The mill at Woking before it was transformed into a printing works

51.

Unwins Sports Day 1908. "Threading the Needle".

52.

SAND AND GRAVEL PITS.

New Crane 1940.   53.

Send has a constantly changing landscape. As its name suggests it has always been a source of sand and gravel. The Enclosure Act of 1803 gave provision for three acres of common land where inhabitants could dig sand for their own use, which they can still do.

The first commercial extractor was probably the nursery gardener Stephen Spooner. In the 1890s his men dug by hand an area between Wharf Lane, Send Road and the canal. Each shovelful was graded for size by throwing it against a mesh screen. He then reclaimed the land with top soil and sludge. He subsequently started excavating between Send Road and Potters Lane where earlier he had had his rhubarb fields. This was left as a small lake where during the 1939-45 war the army tested amphibious vehicles. In the '20s Mr. Spooner charged 6d. a yard for gravel. A new era started in the 1920s with mechanical digging and mechanical transport. The Woking firm of Athertons moved into the area and their pits could be dug to over twenty feet deep. In the early '30s, Hall & Company the Croydon firm, took over the Polesden lane pit and having bought Heath Farm and Prews Farm from Mr. Secrett the market gardener, gravel extraction became one of the area's main industrial activities.

One of the largest areas of extraction has been landscaped and now, as "Papercourt Lake", is used by many species of migrant birds, and for fishing and sailing.

54.

LAUNDRIES.

Mrs. Sale   55a.

55b.

Clothes used to be much more elaborate and they were not made of easy-care, man-made fibres. Most villages had cottage laundries with open drying greens. Ripley had several of these (and pocket money could be earned by pushing a wheel-barrow of laundry from Miss Hook on the Green to Ripley Court School).

Send was unusual for a village in that it had three commercial laundries:— Burt's, Taylor's and Sale's, all working soon after 1900 and into the '20s. Bed linen and staff uniforms were collected in hampers from the larger houses in Send, and from Woking and Guildford as well. Caps and aprons not only had to be starched but also frilled with the goffering tongs. Mrs. Matilda Sale, in Wharf Lane, had a goffering machine, worked by turning a handle, and a central stove with racks for heating the flat irons.

The larger stove, shown here, owned by Bob Whapshott, was made in about 1860 and holds ten irons. His smaller 'tortoise' stove holds about five irons.

56a.

56b.

FARMING.

Woking Broadmead in Send was divided into plots and managed in a way reminiscent of the mediaeval strip system until long after Copyhold was abolished in 1926. No hedges ever divided the strips. It was first ploughed during the Second World War. Hay was grown from January until the 15th August when the beasts, which were branded W.B.M. could be grazed. (Someone, possibly in a fit of parochialism, sawed the letter "W" off the branding iron).

A farren owners' meeting was held once a year to decide on the Broadmead herdsman and to discuss common problems. Under the Broadmead regulations owners were entitled to turn out "one horse, mare or gelding, two cows or beasts of that kind or five sheep for every acre they used, and so in proportion. . . . . ." One owner, Mr. Bayliss, was allowed to graze one horse, two cows and two and a half sheep. His daughter, Margaret, remembers gathering someone else's hay from a neighbouring strip by mistake.

Here is Alf Parsons mounting the load. Note the ear cases for the horses. These were made by May Giles to keep off the flies.

57.

58.

Joe Baigent on a mower in 1931. He was the last Broadmead herdsman. He branded the animals, and checked that the horses had their hind shoes removed.

MARKET GARDENING.

Market gardening became one of Send's chief occupations in the 20th century. Mr. Spooner grew fruit and vegetables to be sold in his sons' shops in Woking and Guildford. It was he who excavated gravel near Potter's Lane as noted on a previous page. Samuel Boorman of Heath Farm cultivated land from the canal right up to the Portsmouth Road, a distance of over a mile, supplying Crosse & Blackwell with peas, raspberries and other produce which were loaded at Clandon Station. Local labour was supplemented by gypsies, camping in the summer, some of their children attending the local school.

59.

60.

Reg Tidy, who worked first for Mr. Boorman then for Mr. Secrett, leading Captain and Senator in 1940.

Gypsy encampment 1881.   61.

Land Girls 1940.   62.

During the Second World War Mr. Secrett, Mr. Boorman's successor at Heath Farm, not only continued to use gypsy labour and built special huts for them, but also employed Land Girls and prisoners-of-war to keep the supply of fruit and vegetables going to Covent Garden.

Gordon Stewart started the British Poultry Development Company at Send Manor. He also reared rare pheasants in his incubators and even hatched an ostrich egg for London Zoo. Harold Giles, the foreman, is seen here feeding the hens.

63.

Mr. Stewart had Great Dane kennels and his dogs and kennel maids often went to County Shows. In 1933 he owned 150 dogs and hoped to breed 200 puppies.

64.

General farming still continued in the area. Horses were only slowly being replaced by machinery. Here is a donkey-powered elevator in the 1940s. Skilled farm hands could plant potatoes evenly and almost as quickly as a machine by rolling them out of the corner of the sack, and older inhabitants can remember seed being hand sown using a fiddle (a box with a seed scattering disk spun by a "bow").

65.

RIVER WEY & THE WEY NAVIGATION.

Stoke Meadows 1908.

66.

The Wey Navigation managed from 1890–1965 by Messrs. William Stevens & Sons carried goods from Weybridge to Godalming. The weigh bills show (amongst other goods) flour being carried from Newark Mill, oak bark to the Tannery and timber to Guildford. During the Second World War the barges went right through to the London docks to collect food. The Wey was operating commercially until 1969 when Mr. Stevens handed it over to The National Trust.

Two horses were usually used in tandem to pull the barges. These were sometimes stabled at Newark Mill or Worsfold Gates.

67.

Four generations of the Grove family worked on the canal. Two of them were Master Carpenters based at Worsfold Gates covering the period 1885–1966. They were responsible for the upkeep of the canal, its banks and locks. Here is the working barge used to hand-dredge the canal and carry the pilings and the new gates they had made.

68.

In the workshop at Worsfold Gates they not only prepared all the wood needed but made the metal work too, including nuts and bolts. There was always a glue pot bubbling on the stove and the smell permeated everywhere.

The workshop cum forge is believed to have been here for over 300 years – since the opening of the Wey Navigation.

69.

70.

Boating Party at Newark in 1886.

71.

The Boathouse at Worsfold Gates hired out all sorts of pleasure craft – skiffs, punts, canoes. Many of the Sunday School, or Girls Friendly Society outings consisted of a trip on the river. Other pleasure craft were allowed to use the canal after payment of a toll. Collection of these tolls was a further task in a very busy life for the canal worker.

Trigg's Lock.

72.

Worsfold Gates, Send, Woking.

Oliver Photo Send

73.

"Go out to the land at Broadmead over which the flood
has been since the grass was cut and before the hay was
made. Six men are turning the hay, some of whom are
working without shoes or stockings. The water stands
on the land and cannot get away".
(Extract from Edward Ryde's diary 8th August 1886)

74.

Looking across to Unwin Brothers over the
flooded Broadmead in 1910.

Send church seen from over the river.

75.

Boys fishing at Sendholme circa 1905.

FAMILY AND CHILDHOOD.

77.

William, Grace, and
Lillian Gunner.

78.

In the early years of this century families were large and there were often as many as thirteen children, the older children helping to look after the younger ones. At a very early age most of them had jobs to do to earn their pocket money – making the paper spills for lighting the fire, cutting the old suits for rag rugs, fetching the jug of milk from the farm before school – and often spilling it – and collecting fire wood.

When asking for a birthday present one child was told "your present is on your feet". Another had her new boots bought out of her money box and she could have what was left over.

Boots with hooks and laces were the usual footwear for both boys and girls. The girls wore pinafores and the boys a celluloid collar that scratched and a cap which had to be raised for greetings.

Toys were usually simple – tops, hoops (iron for the boys, wooden for the girls), and glass 'alleys' – the marble from the neck of Stansfield's lemonade bottles being in great demand. There was no shortage of country activities such as ferreting, egg collecting or fishing for tiddlers.

79.

80.

The Best Baby Competition at a Garden Party in Sendholme.   81.

Although few from the village went away to the seaside in the '20s and '30s, most people said their childhood was happy. They remember family walks along the river and family picnics. Parties and outings were arranged by schools and churches and by several of the larger establishments.

Local brakes and waggons took children to outings such as Wembley, or the Aldershot Tattoo. Occasionally they went further afield by·train. In 1922 one choirboy reported in the Parish Magazine:– "The train advertised to run didn't. We set out to go to Southsea but didn't get there till 6 pm, via Portsmouth and Ryde."

Magic lantern shows were given at Ripley Court and Send Grove, and presents were given at the school Christmas party. One year they had scrapbooks 'tastefully arranged' by Mrs. Sutcliffe and Mrs. Cleverly. They were also sent home with a "bun and an orange".

For the photographer, Archie Marsh wears the popular sailor suit for 'best' in 1918.

82.   83.

SCHOOL DAYS.

84.

The Send National School in 1904 with Lance Rawes the headmaster. Notice the celluloid collars and the Norfolk jackets for older boys, and pinafores for girls. Also notice the younger boys had crochet collars for 'best'.

Many children had a long walk to school, having collected the milk from the farm first, and in the strawberry season Mr. Rawes noted in the Log book that many pupils were sleepy because they had been out picking in the fields since 4 am. In fact holidays were fixed to suit a rural area, in July and at the end of September, the actual dates depending on the state of the crop.

May Day was another holiday. The children with miniature maypoles decorated with hawthorn bunches went round to the larger houses singing –

"May Day is the first of May Give us a penny and we'll run away".

85.   Lance Rawes – headmaster of Send School from 1889-1923, with his wife.

40

86.

Although a grant towards the buildings of both Ripley and Send schools was obtained, the former in 1845 and the latter in 1853, most of the money to build and run the schools was raised by local subscriptions, and each pupil paid a small fee. Later, government grant aid depended first on results, then on attendance figures. Inspectors' reports were often printed in the Parish Magazine. Both schools were fortunate in their headmasters, and these reports were usually good.

The National Schools of both Send and Ripley became too small because of the growing population and the raising of the school leaving age to fourteen in 1918. Further problems arose with evacuees and their staff in the '40s. Sometimes classes alternated morning and afternoon. Overflow classes went to the Drill Hall and the Red Cross Hut in Send, or to the Methodist Hall in Ripley. Both schools closed in 1972.

87.

Send Infants carrying their chairs on their way to the Red Cross Hut in Sandy Lane.

88.

Mr. Berridge started a boarding school in Ryde House at the London end of Ripley High Street in 1860. Ryde House Commercial School was later moved to a larger building at the Guildford end of Ripley and was run by Mr. T. S. Goodman with Mr. Evershed as senior master. Although a co-educational school, the boys and girls separated for meals and spent their pocket money in different shops – the boys in Gibbons next to the church and the girls in Farr's. A slab of Macintosh toffee cost one penny for two ounces. The silver threepenny piece was given out on Saturday, less any halfpenny fines incurred for untidiness.

One pupil, Connie Curtis, said she learnt a form of shorthand 'Sloan Duployan' but found that although it was better and easier than Pitmans most employers expected her to change to the more widely used method.

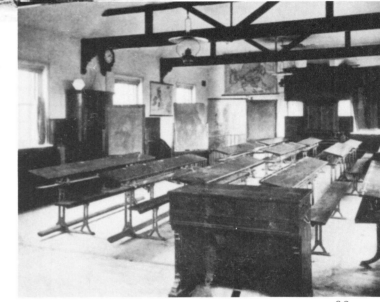

89.

90.

Swimming was taught in the River Wey. There was a hut for changing – though the local children who did not attend the private schools said they had to find a bulrush or two!

They also took boats out on the river.

91.

The wedding of one of the teachers, Miss Emmie Tomkin, to Charles Nokes in 1919. Mr. Goodman is on the extreme left. One of his former pupils called him the "Pied Piper" because the children loved him so much. He used to keep at school children whose parents were abroad even when the fees were no longer forthcoming, and bought them replacement clothes with his own money. The newspaper report of this wedding lists the wedding presents and the donors – a habit which must have cost much heart searching. These gifts were typical of their day:– a silver epergne, an oak crumb tray and brush, a pair of silver mounted vases and a silver mounted butter dish.

Started by Mr. R. M. Pearce in 1893, Ripley Court School was known as the "school for gentlemen's sons". Although it was a boarding school and did not cater for the village it still had an important impact. Many a local boy at the age of fourteen had his first job there – cleaning boots, sharpening knives, tending the lamps in the school-rooms and mowing the cricket pitch. It is still a school but is now co-educational, and has day pupils as well.

92.

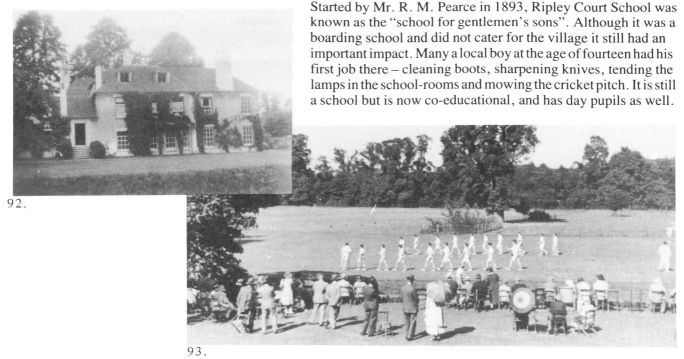

93.

Mrs. Pearce, who continued as headmistress after her husband's death in 1917, also took a very active part in the village and continued to lend the grounds for village celebrations and Sunday School treats.

THE COUNTRY HOUSE.

94.

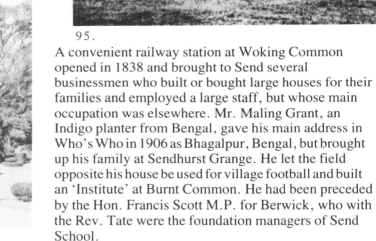

95.

96.

A convenient railway station at Woking Common opened in 1838 and brought to Send several businessmen who built or bought large houses for their families and employed a large staff, but whose main occupation was elsewhere. Mr. Maling Grant, an Indigo planter from Bengal, gave his main address in Who's Who in 1906 as Bhagalpur, Bengal, but brought up his family at Sendhurst Grange. He let the field opposite his house be used for village football and built an 'Institute' at Burnt Common. He had been preceded by the Hon. Francis Scott M.P. for Berwick, who with the Rev. Tate were the foundation managers of Send School.

97. Sendhurst Grange.

98. Mr. W. M. Grant.

99.

The Recorder of Manchester, Sir Joseph Leese, lived at Sendholme and was followed in 1895 by Mr. A. H. Lancaster, a retired paint merchant, pictured above with his wife. Mr. Lancaster endowed the Send Institute and Drill Hall, later called the Lancaster Hall.

Mr. Lancaster hired the Gresham Brass Band from Unwins for parties, and gave his employees the entrance money for the fête. Mrs. Lancaster hired a barge on the river for the school children and threw them handfuls of sweets as they set off.

100.

101.

102.

A few of the household staff of Ockham Park. Samuel Hubbard, the butler, is in the centre
and Mrs. Hawkins, the housekeeper, is dressed in black.

The chief occupation available for women in the earlier part of the century was domestic service. Sendholme and
Sendhurst Grange each employed over twenty people, and Ockham Park had many more, but even smaller homes
would have a housekeeper or cook general. Each member of the female staff would have her own specific tasks, her
own uniform, her own place in the servants' hall and her seat in the church. There were few labour saving devices.
Rooms were ornately furnished. Meals were formal both in the dining room and the servants' hall – so there was much
to do from blacking the grate and filling the oil lamps, to producing elaborate meals for house parties. Despite the
hard labour, a deep attachment was often formed so that many an employee went with them if the family moved.

The running of these large houses depended on a ready supply of labour, but equally the owners gave much in return
to the community in addition to employment. Their names were on all the subscription lists:– for the School Fund,
the Fire Brigade, the District Nurse. Their gardens were opened for the annual fête or flower festival, and on special
occasions such as a Jubilee or Coronation. The Parish Magazine frequently reported parties for the school children
with a magic lantern show, a conjuror, or a Christmas tea.

A fête in the grounds
of Sendholme.

103.

Ockham Park 1870.
(The Lushingtons
in residence).

104.

The Countess of Lovelace was one of the biggest landowners of the area and took a very active interest in Ripley village affairs, although her house pictured above was at Ockham Park. She gave the ground for Ripley churchyard extension, leased the land for the original Church Room and gave land to the village school for the children's gardening lessons. The Foresters' fête used to be held in her grounds, and many of the celebratory processions started or ended in Ockham Park. She was President of the Volunteer Fire Brigade and used to have them to practise fire drill with her own staff – she would be first down a chute attached to the bedroom windows, showing the way for her maids.

105. Mary, Countess of Lovelace. "At Home" – Ockham Park 1935.

106.

Mr. Cleverly of Dunsborough Park, the largest house in Ripley, also did much for the village. He was churchwarden for many years and not only gave the dossal and curtains for the altar, and the sanctuary lamp, but also submitted designs for the chancel floor and for the new side chapel. He formed an indoor rifle club in his grounds and presented the "Silver Spoon" awards for the highest score. In December 1915 he was one of the two chairmen of the local recruiting committee.

107.

Mr. C. F. M. Cleverly.

108.

Some of the outside workers at Dunsborough about 1912. Every year Mrs. Cleverly gave a Christmas party for the children of the staff. One year each child received a Noah's ark full of wooden animals.

WAR

The First World War opened up new opportunities for women. They now served in shops, helped in the smithies, and many worked at Vickers Aircraft establishment in Byfleet – in the cutting room or the paint shop.

In the Second World War those who were 'in service' found it was not a reserved occupation, and this was really the end of the country house era.

109.

Women workers at Vickers in 1920 wearing overalls and caps made out of the same material as that which covered the aircraft wings.

Mounted troops watering their horses at the pond on Ripley Green, circa 1915. One local boy used to slip out to trade his mother's bread – a treat for soldiers after their rations of dry biscuits – for a ride on one of their horses.

110.

111.

The young trees in this picture were planted by Sir Wilfrid Stokes to commemorate the end of the Great War (Sir Wilfrid invented the Stokes Mortar). In the background can be seen Farr's shop where bread was baked in a brick oven that had been heated by burning wood faggots inside it. The wood ash was raked out before the dough lumps were put in on the blade of a long handled shovel. The cottage on the right had not yet been demolished to make way for a coach park behind Bland's garage.

The Home Guard in the Second World War practising on Ripley Green with a Blacker Bombard.

112.

It was believed that Ripley was bombed in September 1940 by mistake for Vickers Works. That was the night when the ferrets got loose in Newark Lane to the consternation of the Air Raid Wardens, and a few days later Tom Buller from the neighbouring house found himself and his bed in a crater in the garden with his watch still ticking on the bed-head.

113.

Prisoners-of-war were housed in Boughton Hall during the First World War, and others were brought in from the Merrow camps to help in drainage schemes and on the farms. During the Second World War some slept in the farm stables and haylofts. In the centre of this picture are two Italian P.O.W's, one of whom still lives locally.

114.

Ripley Fire Brigade on the Green with Johnny Pullen, its first captain, on the left, and Tommy Harding the chief engineer sitting on the left of the engine. It had been formed in 1891 – its patroness was Mary, Countess of Lovelace, with Captain C.M.H. Pearce and Dr. F. E. Pearse as trustees of the subscribers.

The firemen received a fee for each turnout and a charge was made for having your fire put out. New equipment, and also boots and helmets for the men, were bought with funds raised by public subscription. The subscription list was published with names and amounts subscribed – a blatant form of social blackmail.

In 1910 the Countess of Lovelace granted a lease of a site in Rose Lane for a fire station, and Mr. Cleverly of Dunsborough House lent £120 for 12 years for its building costs.

115.

Fire Brigades were in demand for all village processions and for drill competitions such as those at the Sendholme or Ripley Court fêtes. The horse and engine even acted as a wedding vehicle carrying the bridesmaids to church.

116.

Send Fire Brigade in 1914, a year after it was formed. It was under the control of the Parish Council and was funded out of the parish rates.

Joe Baigent in the 1920s. 117.

There was seldom time after they heard the call-boy's bell to don their beautiful uniforms. One Ripley fireman was called out of his daughter's christening, and another ruined his working suit by falling into the slurry pit at Wisley Farm. During the winter their hoses and clothes were draped with icicles. In the summer when there was no hydrant near, they had to use the nearest farm pond and refill it later. For fires on Wisley Common, "Pencil" Brown was given the task of crawling through the pipe that ran under the A3 to take the hose to Bolder Mere.

In the 1940s Ripley Fire Brigade became absorbed into the Auxiliary Fire Service.

Here in 1953 are Firemen Robins, Brewer and Giles, with Mr. Robins' children dressed in the part of the earlier "call-boys".

118.

CRICKET.

This picture of Ripley cricket team was probably taken about 1890.   119.

Ripley Cricket Club was formed in 1743 and played on the village green as it still does.

120.

There were charity matches between the men and the women in aid of the Nursing Fund. The gentlemen had to bat left handed and catch one handed – in 1938 the score was Ladies 110 : Gentlemen 78.

On the right of the picture Dickie Field of the "Half Moon", dressed as a woman, is organizing the collection.

121.

122.

Ernest "Shanger" Cox, the carrier, is helping cut the Green in the 1930s using Collins' delivery van, while Tom Buller, who usually drove the van, is relegated to sitting on the machine. Helpers were not always so willing. The Minutes of 1931 complained that though there were always people to put up the marquee, no-one stayed behind to take it down. There was trouble too when the roller borrowed from Mr. Gatley was returned to him damaged, having been used by many others in the village. Cricket in those days involved the whole village.

123.

In 1945 the New Zealand Services XI, with Roger Blunt as Captain, played against Ripley. A commentary on the match by John Arlott was broadcast to the Services network. This picture is of the winning Ripley team with its President, Sir Oliver Simmonds, centre front. Ripley has continued to play each year against the London New Zealand team.

REGULARS.
W. MAY   CAPTAIN
H. ELLIOTT
G. Mc ONSLOW
G. HILL
H. WINNEY
C. BAIGENT
E. BAIGENT
G. WICKSON
H. JACKMAN
A. STRUDWICK
F. COSTA
UMPIRE : COL. QUILL

THE REST
MR. RAWES HON. SEC.
A. LILLYWHITE
W. SEX
MR. SHIRER
G. PASSINGHAM
T. QUILL
G. HOLE
J. MONERY
B. HARVEY
R. CHARMAN
J. HALE
G. SPENCER GROUNDSMAN

E. TICE   G. HOLE   A. LILLYWHITE   . . . .
COL. QUILL G. PASSINGHAM, J. MONERY T. QUILL G. HILL   H. WINNIE   MR. RAWES G. HARVEY R. CHARMAN . . . . . . J. HALE M. HUGGINS . . . . . . F. HUGGINS
    G. Mc ONSLOW   MR. SHIRER MR. ELLIOTT W. MAY   MR. LANCASTER   E. BAIGENT   F. COSTA . . . . . . T. JACKMAN
F. MILLARD   W. SEX   . . . . A. COLLINS . . . .   C. BAIGENT G. WICKSON H. JACKMAN A. STRUDWICK

124.   An early picture of Send Cricket Club taken in the grounds of Sendholme in 1898.

Whereas Ripley played its matches on the village green, and still does, Send enjoyed the patronage of the owners of Sendholme. In the 1870s Sir Joseph Leese was renowned for his country house cricket. He, his six sons and guests made up a team against visiting house teams, and a cricket-playing gardener of his could pass the summer doing very little work! Sir Joseph had a marl pitch laid out in his grounds and allowed the village to use it, and this Mr. Lancaster continued to do.

Send Cricket Club still play on the leased pitch, now with a pavilion which the members built themselves in 1950.

Send used to have a cricket week in which most of the village participated – the wives making tea in a huge urn over an open fire. One popular match was the Married v Single.

125.

Cricket at Sendholme with the new pavilion in the background.

126.

In 1220 Henry III granted the Priory of Newark the right to hold a fair at Ripley on July 22nd. In living memory it lasted a full week and continued to be held right up to 1939. From all accounts it was one of the highlights of the year. There were games of skill such as hitting the weight, or competing in the wrestling booths. Roundabouts, worked by steam engines, were brought by Smith & Whittles or Mrs. Thomas & Company.

The bonfire fancy dress procession used to be held in daylight and in this one in the 1920s it is headed by Mr. Albert Daws and Mrs. Agate as a mock bride and groom.

127.

The bonfire used to be built by the children of the village – the boys cut the 'fuzzies' and the girls dragged the tied bundles – but when in the '30s it was prematurely set alight (said by the villagers to be by the students of Wisley) the adults took over. Here a huge bonfire is being built with Ernest Cox, the carrier, up the stack and his carrier's van on the right.

128.

Below is the procession of the Order of Foresters in Ripley High Street in 1920 on its way to Ockham Park fête where, with a flower show, a band, and country dancing as part of the festival, they raised funds, as did many other Friendly Societies formed in the 19th century to help in times of sickness and unemployment.

129.

ORGANIZATIONS AND OUTINGS.

Because there was no National Health Service and very little help with unemployment, Coal Clubs, Clothing Clubs and Slate Clubs were important. Many of the pubs ran a Slate Club in which people could invest small weekly savings. Their day outings were often the only holiday people took.

Two Slate Club outings of 1920. The one above was organised by the "New Inn", Send; the one below by the "White Hart" Ripley.

130.

131.

132.

The Ripley Girls Friendly Society was formed in 1878 with Miss Onslow as President, and first Mrs. Dibble of the "Anchor", then Mrs. Pearce of Ripley Court as Chairman. They entered handcraft exhibitions and choir festivals and played cricket on Ripley Court field. Here is an outing in 1925. Often their annual treats were closer to home – in the garden of Newark Mill or of Pyrford Place, or having a picnic tea near Bolder Mere.

133.

The dedication of the new Ripley British Legion Standard in 1955. To the left the Chairman Mr. Brown, and to the right Bert Hockley, and the standard bearer. The Ripley Royal British Legion branch was formed in 1921. The Send Royal British Legion branch in 1920. In 1930 Miss Evelyn Lancaster of Sendholme organized a fund "to give aid to ex-servicemen in need of relief".

FUN AND GAMES.

Both villages seem to have made much fun for themselves.

134.

This Farman bi-plane caused great excitement by landing at Broadmead in 1910 so that the owner Graham White could answer a summons at Woking Magistrates Court for speeding in his car.

In the '20s it was a great thrill to sit inside an aeroplane which you could do for sixpence. In the '30s 'joy rides' were available on the Broadmead and near Sussex Farm.

135.

Send had a fine group of bellringers and a fine set of bells. They are performing here in the "Saddlers Arms" one Christmas, collecting for the Waifs and Strays. Tom Faithfull is the one in the centre, and the leader George Baigent is on the extreme left.

136.

For all state occasions in Send the day used to start with the old custom of firing the anvils at Sex's forge. They were fired in 1900 following the Relief of Mafeking, and in 1911 for the Coronation of George V, and also for the Coronation of George VI in 1937. The holes in the base of the upturned anvil were filled with gunpowder and the charge was exploded with a lighted fuse. After that the sports, country dancing and feasting started.

137.

In the afternoons at Send were the games – ringing the bull, tug of war and throwing the quoit. This picture was taken in 1911 during the celebrations for the Coronation of George V.

Ripley usually started with a fancy dress procession. To the left is one, representing all the colonies, on its way to the White Hart meadows for the Coronation of George V.

138.

The procession in the picture on the right is for the Coronation of Elizabeth in 1953.

139.

George V's Jubilee in 1935 was also celebrated in both villages. Here on the left is the model train made by Mr. Methold on which he gave free rides to the children.

140.

141.

And as in the rest of England, victory in 1945 was
celebrated by 'street parties'.